Leafy Adventure

Arti Mishra

BookLeaf Publishing

Presentation by *BookLeaf Publishing*

Web: www.bookleafpub.com

E-mail: info@bookleafpub.com

ISBN: 9789363304758

First edition 2024

Dedication

To my mother,
the heart and hands behind my love for gardening.

From her, I learned that growth is not just in the plants we nurture, but also in the patience, love, and care we give to everything we touch.

She is an artist who brings life to everything – whether it's the strokes of her paintbrush, the warmth of her stitches, the flavor of her homemade pickles, or the vibrant garden she always shares a picture of in the morning.

As the wife of a soldier, she has rooted our family with strength and grace, and it's from her that I've inherited this passion for growing.

Thank you for teaching me the art of growing, both in plants and in life.

This book is for you, and for all the ways you continue to inspire me.

Acknowledgements

Writing this book has been quite the journey – one that I absolutely couldn't have done alone. So, let me take a moment to thank the people in my life who helped make this happen. First, to my mother—you've been my constant inspiration and gardening guru. Thank you for always being there, answering all my panicked "Why is this plant dying and what seed can I grow now?" calls, and for your endless wisdom in both the garden and life. From you, I learned that patience, much like watering a plant, can yield the most beautiful growth – even if it takes a bit longer than expected.

My better half, Raj, for accepting that 50% of my household is now Garden related and eventually transforming into a plant lover himself. He is the best pruner I have. He knows well that if I am upset or stressed out, gardening is the only thing that will bounce me back. He often says that gardening is my meditation!

To my brothers Vivek and Vikas and my sister-in-laws, Harsha and Shilpi – you've witnessed firsthand the gradual transformation of our home into what I lovingly call "paradise." Thank you for putting up with all the pots, the endless bags of soil, and the occasional (okay, frequent) plant-related messes that somehow seem to take over every available surface. Your support and tolerance for my green obsession – means the world to me.

And all of you are Gardeners today – better than me!

Namo – our little champ who knows early morning is watering time for plants, picking the spray bottle as soon as you come to terrace and slowly watering the plants. I am sure these plants love you too.

To my gardener friends Anu and Satya – you know who you are. Thank you for cheering me and gifting me so many plants, pretending to listen when I wouldn't stop asking about plants from your Garden, and for never laughing (too hard) when I brought home yet another "must-have" houseplant.

To my editor – thank you for carefully pruning my words, much like weeding a garden. You kept me from wandering too far off into the wild and brought clarity where I might have created a jungle. This book is a thousand times better because of your hard work, so thank you for bringing order to the chaos.

To the kind folks at plant nurseries and garden centers, especially the one from Hadapsar – owned by Amol – thank you for indulging my endless questions and for allowing me to explore your jumbo nursery in Pune, almost every weekend.

And finally, to the endless cups of tea that fuelled my early-morning writing sessions, and the audiobooks that kept me going when I hit the dreaded “writer’s block” – I couldn’t have done it without you. You may not have watered any plants, but you certainly kept me writing.

And to you, dear reader – thank you for picking up this book. I hope it brings a little more green into your life (and maybe even a few “Why is this plant dying?” moments).

Here’s to your Leafy Adventure!

Contents

Introduction

Plants are more than just decorative pieces or sources of oxygen; they are living beings with the power to transform our spaces and our lives. They teach us patience, offer us companionship, and connect us to the earth in a way that nothing else can.

Plants are everywhere—in our homes, gardens, parks, and even in our kitchens. But how often do we stop to appreciate the subtle yet profound ways they impact our lives? The green leaves that photosynthesize sunlight into energy are, in many ways, the life force of our planet. They purify the air we breathe, provide us with food and medicine, and offer a sense of tranquility that few other things can.

Welcome to a world where love for plants isn't just a hobby—it's a way of life. Whether you're here because you've always admired the lush greenery in others' homes or you're already knee-deep in potting soil, this book is your gateway to a lifelong love affair with plants.

In this book, we'll explore the magic of plants and how they can bring joy and peace into your life.

This book is for anyone who wants to deepen their connection with plants. Whether you're a complete beginner or an expert gardener, there's always something new to learn in the world of plants. We'll take you on a journey that starts with the basics and gradually leads you to the heights of expert gardening.

HOW TO MAKE BEST OF THIS BOOK

For your easy navigation, this book has three sections. Each section is tailored for readers at different stages: those who just want to begin their plant journey, the ones who are already happy plant parents, and those who are deep into gardening.

Section 1

> **The Beginner's Green Thumb:** If you have just made up your mind to get a few plants to your home and you're new to the world of gardening, this section is for you. We'll cover the basics, from choosing your first plants to creating a simple green space in your home. You will learn to grow resilient plants and

watch them become your companions full of love and life.

Section 2

Growing with Confidence: After getting friendly with your first few roommates and making them part of your life, you feel ready to take your gardening skills to the next level; this section will explore more diverse plant species that you can add to your space. You will learn to train your plants to live without you when you are away. You would also learn to tackle common challenges, and tips for creating beautiful plant displays.

Section 3

Mastering the Green Arts: For the seasoned gardener, this section dives into advanced techniques, from hydroponics to cultivating rare plants. You will also become a good plant communicator and can easily spot challenges of your plants. You'll learn how to design both indoor and outdoor gardens and give back to nature through sustainable practices.

Section 1: The Beginner's Green Thumb

Chapter I
Falling in Love with Plants

Every great love story has a beginning, and for many of us, the journey with plants starts with a simple realization: plants make life better. It might begin with something as small as receiving a gift—a tiny succulent from a friend—or perhaps a sudden urge to brighten up your living space with a bit of greenery. Maybe you were inspired by a beautiful garden or admired a plant at a hotel or a café. Whatever the reason, the first step is always the most important: deciding to bring a plant into your life.

At first, it might seem like just another thing to take care of, but plants are so much more than that. They're living, breathing companions that respond to your care, attention, and love. When you water a plant, place it in just the right spot, and watch it soak up the sunlight, you're not just maintaining it—you're nurturing life. This act of nurturing can be deeply fulfilling. There's something truly special about watching a plant grow, seeing new leaves unfurl, or witnessing the first bloom of a flower. You read the plant's smile; it's like magic, and it reminds us of the beauty and vitality of life. It also teaches us patience, as growth takes time, and the rewards are well worth the wait.

But where to start? The world of plants is vast and can feel a bit overwhelming, especially when you're just beginning. There are so many types of plants, each with its own needs, preferences, and personality. Some thrive in the sun, while others prefer the shade. Some need frequent watering, while others do better when left alone. But don't worry—every plant lover starts somewhere. Whether you have a green thumb or are completely new to the idea, this book is here to guide you through those first steps.

Imagine you're stepping into a garden for the first time, unsure of where to begin. Maybe you'll start with something simple, like a small indoor plant that doesn't require much attention. Or perhaps you'll dive right in with a few different plants, experimenting to see which ones thrive in your environment. The important thing is to start. As you learn more about plants, you'll discover what works best for you and your space.

You'll make mistakes—everyone does—but each mistake is a learning experience that brings you closer to becoming a confident plant parent.

So, let's begin this journey together. Let's explore the joys of growing, caring for, and loving plants. By the end of this book, you'll not only have a collection of beautiful plants but also a deeper connection with nature and a greater appreciation for the simple, yet profound, act of nurturing life.

Chapter 2
Choosing Your First Plants

Choosing your first plants can be a lot of fun, but it's completely normal to feel a bit overwhelmed by the sheer number of options. With so many different types of plants, how do you know which ones are the best fit for you? The good news is, you don't have to know everything right away. The key is to start simple. You'll want to look for plants that are low maintenance, forgiving, and well-suited to the environment you can offer them. Think of it like starting a new hobby—begin with something easy and build your confidence from there.

So, where to begin? Let's talk about some beginner-friendly plants that are perfect for new plant parents. These plants are like the friendly, patient teachers of the plant world. They don't require too much fuss, and they'll give you a little grace if you don't get everything right the first time.

Start your indoor-plants journey with one of these 4 plants:

A. SNAKE PLANTS

If you're looking for a plant that's practically impossible to kill, let me introduce you to the Snake Plant. Seriously, this might be one of the easiest plants to care for, making it perfect for beginners. Whether you're someone who's always on the go, a bit forgetful when it comes to watering, or just new to plant care, the Snake Plant is your new best friend. It's tough, resilient, and looks great in any space.

Why the Snake Plant is So Easy to Care For

The Snake plant is famous for being absolutely low maintenance. It has superpowers to tolerate different kinds of environments. Got a dark corner in your room? No problem—the Snake Plant can handle low light. Have a spot that gets a bit of sunlight? Great! The Snake Plant will soak it up, but it won't get upset if there's not enough light. And watering? You can almost forget about it. Snake Plants store water in their thick, upright leaves, so they don't need much care at all. In fact, they are happy when you let the soil dry out completely between waterings.

It's almost like the Snake Plant was made for people who might forget about their plants from time to time (and let's be honest, we've all been there). With very little effort, this plant will thrive and add a touch of greenery to your home. They are perfect to begin your leafy adventure!

Types of Snake Plants You'll Love

There's more than one type of Snake Plant, so you have some fun options to choose from. Here are a few of the most popular varieties, all of which are just as easy to care for:

Variegated Snake Plant:

This is the classic Snake Plant with tall, sword-like leaves that have green centers and yellow edges. It's the one you'll see most often, and it's great for making a bold statement in any room. Its upright growth makes it perfect for small spaces because it grows tall rather than wide.

Mother-in-Law's Tongue:

This type has tall, dark green leaves with lighter green stripes. It's sleek, simple, and very forgiving. This one's perfect if you're looking for a plant that doesn't demand too much attention but still looks sharp. Don't know why it's called Mother-in-Law's Tongue, I think the better word would be Pole-like Snake Plant, isn't it?

Cylinder Snake Plant:

Want something a little different? The Cylinder Snake Plant has round, tube-like leaves that grow straight up or can be braided for a cool look. It's just as easy to care for as its flatter-leafed cousins, but it adds a unique twist to your plant collection.

Moonshine Snake Plant:

This Snake Plant variety has silvery-green leaves that look a bit lighter than the others. It gives off a soft, almost calming vibe and can brighten up any room. Like the rest, it's tough and will thrive with very little care.

'Whale Fin' Snake Plant:

As the name suggests, this one has large, broad leaves that resemble a whale's fin. It's a bit more dramatic and eye-catching, but don't worry—it's still super easy to care for. It grows a little slower but makes a big impact.

How to Care for Your Snake Plant

Snake Plants practically take care of themselves! Let's go over the basics of how to keep your Snake Plant happy and healthy.

1. Light:

Snake Plants are super flexible when it comes to light. They thrive in bright, indirect light, but they can also handle lower light conditions, like a dim corner of your room. This makes them perfect for just about any space. If you happen to have a sunny window, that's great too—they'll love it there.

2. Watering:

One of the few ways to hurt a Snake Plant is by overwatering it, so this is where the "less is more" rule really applies. Let the soil dry out completely between waterings. In the warmer months, you can water it about once every two to three weeks. In the colder months, you can stretch it out even to a month. It's better to underwater than to overwater with these guys.

3. Soil:

Snake Plants aren't picky about soil, but they do prefer well-draining soil. This helps make sure their roots don't sit in water, which could lead to root rot.

4. Temperature:

Snake Plants do best in temperatures between 60-85°F (16-29°C). As long as you keep them away from freezing temperatures, they'll be happy indoors or even outside.

5. Humidity:

Good news—Snake Plants aren't fussy about humidity. They'll do just fine in regular household humidity levels, so there's no need to mist them or worry about moisture in the air.

6. Fertilizing:

You don't need to fertilize your Snake Plant. Just once during the growing season (spring and summer) is more than enough. A vermicompost/manure will do the trick.

Why You'll Love Having a Snake Plant

The Snake Plant isn't just easy to care for—it's also great for improving the air in your home. Studies have shown that Snake Plants can help remove toxins from the air, making your space healthier. They're also wonderful for adding a touch of green to any space.

Plus, Snake Plants grow slowly, so you won't need to worry about repotting them often. They're content to stay in the same pot for years, making them even more low maintenance.

The Snake Plant is the ultimate beginner plant. It's beautiful, tough, and incredibly forgiving. If you're someone who worries about keeping plants alive, this is the perfect plant to start with. And even if you're a seasoned plant lover, the Snake Plant adds a classic, elegant touch to any space.

So go ahead—bring a Snake Plant into your home and enjoy the ease and beauty it brings!

B. SUCCULENTS

Begin your journey of love with Succulents. They are a fantastic choice for beginners. Succulents come in all sorts of shapes and sizes, from tiny, round ones to tall and spiky ones. The best part? They need very little water to survive. If you sometimes forget to water your plants, succulents will forgive you. All they really ask for is plenty of bright light—like a sunny windowsill—and they'll be happy.

Here are 6 succulents that are perfect for beginners:

Aloe Vera:

Aloe vera is one of the most well-known succulents, and for good reason. Not only is it easy to care for, but it also has practical uses—its gel can be used to soothe minor burns and skin irritations. Regular application on skin and hair makes them healthier. Aloe vera has thick, spiky leaves that store water, so you don't need to water it very often. In fact, overwatering is one of the only ways you can harm this plant. It does well in bright spots, like near a window, and should be watered every couple of weeks, or when the soil is completely dry. The leaves turn gray to bluish when it is kept in dark. It's a resilient plant that rewards you with both beauty and utility.

Jade Plant:

The Jade Plant is a symbol of good luck and prosperity, and it's also incredibly easy to care for. Its thick, oval-shaped leaves have a shiny, almost jade-like appearance and so the name. Native to Africa, Jade plants thrive in bright light. Place them near a sunny window where they can soak up some rays. Like most succulents, they don't need frequent watering. Wait until the soil is completely dry before giving it a good soak, and then let it dry out again before the next watering. Over time, Jade Plants can grow into small, tree-like shapes with thick branches, adding a unique charm to your space.

Echeveria:

Echeveria succulents are known for their stunning rosette shapes, which look almost like flowers. They come in a variety of colors, from pale green to deep purple, and can make any windowsill or shelf look more lively. Echeverias love bright, indirect light, so keep them near a window where they can get plenty of sunlight without being scorched. Water them sparingly—every two to three weeks—when the soil feels dry to the touch. With minimum care, they'll reward you with their beautiful, symmetrical growth.

Zebra Plant:

If you're looking for a small, striking succulent, the Zebra Plant is a great choice. It has dark green leaves with white, horizontal stripes that resemble the pattern of a zebra. The Zebra Plant is perfect for beginners because it's low-maintenance and doesn't require much attention. It prefers bright, indirect light, so it'll do well in a spot that gets filtered sunlight. Water it once the soil has completely dried out, and avoid letting water sit in the leaves corner and between the leaves to prevent rot. It's compact, peculiar, unrealistically real and easy-to-grow companion for you.

Burro's Tail:

Burro's Tail is a trailing succulent, which means its fleshy, beaded leaves cascade down like a tail, making it perfect for hanging planters or high shelves. While it might look delicate, burro's tail is surprisingly hardy. Like other succulents, it doesn't need frequent watering—just make sure the soil is dry before giving it a drink. Place it in bright, indirect light and avoid touching the leaves too much, as they can be fragile and fall off easily. With a little care, it will grow long, trailing stems irresistible to touch creating a beautiful, flowing effect.

Panda Plant:

The Panda Plant is a fuzzy, unique-looking succulent with soft, silvery leaves that have brownish-red tips. Its velvety texture makes it a fun and interesting addition to any plant collection. Panda plants do best in bright, indirect light and are quite drought-tolerant. Water them 2-3 weeks, allowing the soil to dry out completely between waterings. They're perfect for beginners who want something a little different. As long as you provide them with the little less than bright light and avoid overwatering, they'll thrive in your home.

Each of these succulents offers something different, but they all share a common trait: they're easy to care for and perfect for beginners.

Remember, the most important thing with succulents is to avoid overwatering and making sure you don't wet their leaves while watering as that can be devastating for the little ones. With just these two tips, your succulents will thrive and bring a touch of nature into your home!

C. ZZ PLANT

If you're just starting out with plants or you're looking for something that practically takes care of itself, the ZZ Plant is your perfect match.

The common name comes from its scientific name Zamioculcas zamiifolia whose both initials are Z- how easy and unique and at the same time a hardy one.

It's like the friendly, reliable neighbor who's always there for you, no matter what. This plant is not only easy to grow, but it also looks great and adds a touch of green to any room. ZZ plant is a fantastic choice for beginner plant lovers.

If you want to get fancy, ZZ plant is a superstar in the plant world, especially for those new to plant care. Its leaves shine like they've just come out of some wonder spa and the dark green color gives it a special attractive feature. It's tough, forgiving, and doesn't ask for much. ZZ Plant is perfect for you.

1. Tough as Nails:

ZZ Plants are incredibly resilient. They can handle a lot of neglect, which means they're perfect if you're a busy person or if you sometimes forget to water your plants. They can go weeks without water and still look fabulous.

2. Low Light Tolerance:

Do you have a spot in your home that doesn't get a lot of sunlight? No worries! The ZZ Plant can thrive in low light conditions. It's a great choice for rooms with little natural light, like offices or north-facing rooms or even your bathroom.

3. Minimal Maintenance:

With the ZZ Plant, there's no need for constant fussing. It doesn't require frequent repotting or special fertilizers. As long as you keep it in a well-draining pot and give it a bit of water every now and then, it will be perfectly happy.

How to Care for Your ZZ Plant

Caring for a ZZ Plant is as easy as pie. Here's a simple guide to make sure your ZZ Plant stays healthy and happy:

1. Light:

ZZ Plants are incredibly adaptable when it comes to light. They prefer bright, indirect light, but they can also tolerate low light. So, whether you have a sunny spot or a more shaded area, your ZZ Plant will manage just fine. The learning agility quotient of this plant is an inspiration to draw from!! Avoid placing it in direct sunlight for long periods, as this can scorch the leaves.

2. Watering:

Here's where the ZZ Plant really shines. It's very drought-tolerant and prefers to be on the dry side. Water it only when the soil has completely dried out. In general, you'll need to water it about every 2-3 weeks or even once a month is perfectly fine for a ZZ. In the winter, you can even stretch this out a bit longer. Overwatering is one of the few ways you can harm your ZZ Plant, so it's better to let it dry out a bit too much than to water it too often.

3. Soil:

The ZZ Plant is not picky about soil, but it does prefer well-draining soil. A general-purpose potting mix works well, especially if it has some added sand or perlite to improve drainage. You don't need to worry about it being too fussy about soil types—just make sure it's not heavy or waterlogged.

4. Temperature:

ZZ Plants are pretty easy-going when it comes to temperature. They thrive in temperatures between 65-75°F (18-24°C). They don't like it too cold, so keep them away from drafty windows or doors, especially in the winter.

5. Humidity:

No need to worry about humidity levels with the ZZ Plant. It's quite tolerant of standard indoor humidity levels, so you don't need to mist it or place it on a pebble tray. It's a great choice for any indoor environment.

6. Fertilizing:

You don't need to fertilize your ZZ Plant often. Use vermicompost once a year in its pot mix and it will be a content plant in your home. The ZZ Plant is not a hungry plant and will be just fine with minimal feeding.

The ZZ Plant isn't just easy to care for; it's also a great air purifier. It can help remove toxins like xylene, toluene, and benzene from the air, making your space a bit healthier. Plus, its sleek, modern look fits in with just about any decor style, from contemporary to traditional.

One of the best things about the ZZ Plant is that it's a great conversation starter. People will be curious about its unique look and will marvel at how you've managed to keep such a beautiful plant alive with minimal effort.

If you're new to plant care or simply want a plant that doesn't demand a lot of attention, the ZZ Plant is the perfect choice. It's forgiving, stylish, and almost impossible to kill. With just a little basic care, it will thrive and brighten up any room. So go ahead—get yourself a ZZ Plant and enjoy the effortless beauty it brings to your home!

D. MONEY PLANT

If you're looking for a plant that's both easy to care for and incredibly charming, let me introduce you to the world of Money Plant, also known as Pothos. If you ask any Indian about Pothos, you will get a puzzled "What's that??" kind of response. However, once you explain the plant, their response will change to, "Oh, the Money Plant!!" Yes, it happens only in India!! Money plant is every household possession here.

This plant is like the friend you can always count on—easygoing, adaptable, and ready to brighten up any space. Whether you're a beginner plant lover or someone who's just looking for a low-maintenance green friend, the Money Plant is the perfect plant to fall in love with.

Money plant plants are incredibly forgiving, which is why they're so perfect for people who are new to plant care. They're not fussy about light, they don't need frequent watering, and they can even grow in water! If you've ever struggled with keeping plants alive, Money plant is your option.

Types of Money plant

One of the best things about Money plant is its versatility. There are several types to choose from, each with its own unique look.

Here's a quick guide to the most popular varieties:

Golden Money plant:

The Golden Money plant is the classic variety you'll often see in homes and offices. Its heart-shaped leaves are a vibrant green with golden-yellow marbling. This plant is not just easy to care for but also adds a beautiful touch of color to any room. It's great for hanging baskets or trailing down from shelves.

Marble Queen Money plant:

If you love a more variegated look, the Marble Queen Money plant is a stunning choice. Its leaves are a mix of green and creamy white, resembling marble. This variety is perfect if you want a plant with a bit more visual interest and elegance. It thrives in similar conditions as the Golden Money plant and looks gorgeous in both hanging pots and as a tabletop plant.

Neon Money plant:

The Neon Money plant lives up to its name with bright, yellowish green leaves that practically glow. This plant adds a pop of vibrant color to any space and can really stand out in a room with neutral tones. It's just as easy to care for as the other types and can thrive in a range of light conditions.

Manjula Money plant:

The Manjula Money plant is known for its unique, textured leaves with intricate patterns of white, silver, and green. It's a bit more exotic looking and adds a touch of flair to any plant collection. It's still beginner-friendly and works well in similar care conditions as the other Money plant varieties.

Silver Satin Money plant:

The Silver Satin Money plant features dark green leaves with a silvery sheen, adding a sleek, modern touch to any space. It's equally easy to care for. A less common variety amongst all kinds of Money Plants, this plant is great for those who want something understated yet stylish.

How to Care for Your Money plant

Caring for a Money plant is as easy as it gets. Here's a simple guide to keeping your plant happy and healthy:

1. Light:

Money plants are very adaptable when it comes to light. They thrive in bright, indirect light but can also tolerate low light conditions. This makes them perfect for rooms with varying light levels. Just avoid placing them in direct sunlight, as this can scorch their leaves.

2. Watering:

One of the best things about Money plant is how forgiving it is with watering. Allow the top inch or so of soil to dry out before watering again.

During the growing season (spring and summer), you might need to water once a week, but in the winter, you can water less frequently. If you forget to water, don't worry; it will remind you by its droopy leaves. As soon as you water it, your Money plant will bounce back quickly.

3. Soil:

Money plants aren't picky about soil. A regular potting mix with good drainage will work just fine. You can also add some perlite or sand to improve drainage, which helps prevent root rot.

4. Temperature:

Money plants prefer temperatures between 60-80°F (15-27°C). They're quite tolerant of temperature fluctuations, but it's best to keep them away from extreme temperatures.

5. Humidity:

Money plants do well in average household humidity. You don't need to worry about misting them or using a humidity tray. They'll thrive in normal indoor conditions.

6. Fertilizing:

Feed your Money plant with vermicompost once every 1-2 months during the growing season. This helps keep it healthy and encourages new growth, giving the plant a playful look.

One of the coolest things about Money plant is that it can grow just as well in water as it does in soil. This makes it a great choice for those who want to try hydroponic growing. Simply place cuttings in a vase or jar filled with water, and you'll see roots begin to form in a few weeks. Change the water every couple of weeks to keep it fresh, and you'll have a thriving, beautiful plant growing in a water container. It's a fun and an easy way to enjoy your Money plant and watch it flourish.

The Money plant is more than just an easy-to-care plant; it's also a versatile and stylish addition to any home. Its trailing vines and heart-shaped leaves create a lush, vibrant look that can transform any space. Plus, its ability to grow in water means you can experiment with different display options and enjoy the plant's beauty in a variety of ways.

Whether you're a new plant lover or a seasoned green thumb, the Money plant is sure to win your heart. It's forgiving, adaptable, and always ready to bring a touch of green into your life. So go ahead, give Money plant a try and see how this charming plant can brighten up your home!

If you're ready to embrace the bright, sunny spots in your home, a few sun-loving plants are perfect for you to add to your bright spaces to further make it brighter.

For beginners, sun-loving plants are not only beautiful but also fairly easy to care for. Start your outdoor plant journey with these 5 plants that are almost impossible to kill:

A. Purple Heart -Spiderwort

If you're on the lookout for a plant that's as easy to care for as it is stunning, let me introduce you to the Purple-Heart Spiderwort. This plant is like a splash of purple sunshine for your home, and it's perfect for beginners who want to enjoy the beauty of plants without the stress of complicated care routines.

It's a plant that thrives on simplicity and sun, making it a joy to grow and maintain. Its bold purple leaves are not only eye-catching but also incredibly easy to manage, which means less worry for you and more time to enjoy its beauty. One of the first things you'll notice about the Purple-Heart Spiderwort is its vibrant color. The leaves are a rich, deep purple that adds a pop of color to any space. It's like having a piece of the sunset right in your home. As the plant grows, it forms a lovely, cascading effect, which makes it a fantastic choice for hanging baskets or as a trailing plant on shelves.

Taking care of the Purple-Heart Spiderwort is incredibly straightforward. Here's a simple guide to keep your plant happy and thriving:

1. Light:

This plant absolutely loves the sun! Place your Purple-Heart Spiderwort in a spot where it can bask in bright, indirect light. It can also handle a bit of direct sunlight, which makes it perfect for a sunny windowsill or a bright room. If you give it the light it craves, you'll be rewarded with vibrant, healthy foliage.

2. Watering:

The Purple-Heart Spiderwort is pretty low-maintenance when it comes to watering. Allow the top inch or so of soil to dry out between waterings. Overwatering can lead to root rot, so it's better to err on the side of less frequent watering. In general, water it every 2-4 weeks.

3. Soil:

This plant isn't picky about soil, but it prefers the well-draining kind. A standard potting mix will work just fine. You can also mix in a bit of perlite or sand to improve drainage, which helps keep the roots healthy and happy.

4. Temperature:

The Purple-Heart Spiderwort enjoys average room temperatures ranging from 15-45°C. It's best to keep it away from cold drafts or sudden temperature changes. This will help ensure it stays in top condition and continues to thrive.

5. Humidity:

No need to worry about humidity with this plant. The Purple-Heart Spiderwort does well in average household humidity. You don't need to mist it or use a humidity tray. Just give it a sunny spot, and it will be content.

The Purple-Heart Spiderwort is more than just a pretty face. It's a plant that does well with minimal attention, which means it's perfect for busy people or those new to plant care. Plus, its unique color and trailing growth habit add a touch of elegance and charm to any place. Mine didn't even budge for water for 3 months when I moved cities and was super happy being the brightest purple color, untouched!

Whether you're setting up a new plant collection or simply looking for a low-maintenance beauty to brighten up your space, the Purple-Heart Spiderwort is a wonderful choice. Its sun-loving nature and vibrant purple leaves make it a plant that you'll enjoy watching grow and thrive with very little effort on your part.

So go ahead, bring a Purple-Heart Spiderwort and let it work its magic. You'll love how it adds a splash of color and joy to your life with just a little sunlight and no care!

B. Moses in the Cradle

If you're looking for a plant that's as intriguing as it is easy to care for, let me introduce you to the Moses in the Cradle. This plant is like a little piece of drama and beauty rolled into one, making it an excellent choice for beginners who want a stunning yet low-maintenance companion. When I first learned about it around 10 years ago, I couldn't believe its color—variegated greens on top and purple at the bottom of leaves, so I got just one for home, thinking it would be fragile and tough to care for. As I learned about the strengths of this beauty, I realized that it's one of the most resilient sun-loving plants that I know exists.

It is a fantastic choice for anyone new to the plant world. With its unique purple green appearance and minimal care requirements, it's a plant that's sure to catch your eye and make your plant care journey a breeze. It's the kind of plant that thrives with little fuss, making it a great addition to any home.

The Moses in the Cradle stands out with its striking, folded leaves that resemble a cradle or a boat—hence the name. These leaves have a glossy green exterior with a dramatic purple underside, adding a touch of elegance and color to any space. As the plant matures, it produces small, inconspicuous flowers nestled within the folds of the leaves, creating a delightful surprise for those who take a closer look.

Taking care of the Moses in the Cradle is as simple as it gets. Here's a straightforward guide to keeping your plant happy and healthy:

1. Light:

This plant loves the sun! Place your Moses in the Cradle in a spot where it can soak up bright, direct light. It can handle a bit of indirect sunlight as well, so a sunny windowsill or a bright room is a great sport for it too. Not that it won'tt thrive in partial shade, low light or no light, as the color of the plant will simply adjust itself to the new environment. But, the more light it gets, the more vibrant its colors will be.

2. Watering:

Moses in the Cradle is quite forgiving when it comes to watering. Allow the top inch or so of soil to dry out between waterings. It's better to err on the side of less frequent watering, as overwatering can lead to root rot. Water it every 2-3 weeks, or whenever the soil feels dry. This plant can handle a bit of neglect, making it perfect for busy plant lovers.

3. Soil:

This plant isn't picky about soil but prefers a well-draining mix. A standard potting soil works well, especially if you mix in a bit of perlite or sand to improve drainage. Good drainage is key to keeping the roots healthy and preventing waterlogged soil.

The Moses in the Cradle is more than just an easy-care plant; it's a conversation starter. Its unique leaf structure and striking colors make it a standout in any plant collection. It adds a touch of exotic flair and visual interest to your space, without demanding much attention.

Whether you're new to plant care or just looking for a reliable and beautiful plant to add to your home, the Moses in the Cradle is a wonderful choice. Its sun-loving nature and minimal care requirements make it a joy to grow and maintain. Plus, its distinctive appearance will bring a touch of intrigue and elegance to your indoor garden.

So go ahead, welcome the Moses in the Cradle into your home. With its easy care and striking beauty, it's sure to become a cherished part of your plant family!

C. Song of India

Have you ever seen a plant that looks like it was painted by nature herself? If not, meet the Song of India. This beauty, with its striking green leaves edged in creamy yellow, is like having a piece of art in your home. But don't let its exotic look fool you—this plant is just as easy to care for as it is beautiful.

The Song of India is perfect for plant lovers of all levels, especially beginners. It's not demanding and can tolerate a bit of neglect, which makes it a forgiving choice for those still learning the ropes. Plus, its long, sword-like leaves give off a tropical vibe that makes any room feel like a mini paradise.

This plant grows in clusters, with new shoots popping out from the stem. And while the name suggests it sings (imagine that!), its charm is silent but oh-so-powerful.

The Song of India may look fancy, but it's surprisingly low maintenance.

1. Light:

Like most tropical plants, it loves bright direct and indirect light. But if you don't have that perfect spot, don't worry! It can adapt to lower light conditions too. The brighter the light, though, the more vibrant its colors will be.

2. Water:

This plant thrives on a schedule that doesn't overwhelm you. Water it when the top inch of soil is dry to the touch. Don't drown it—its roots prefer a little drying out between drinks.

3. Humidity:

Although it's a tropical plant, the Song of India won't demand a humidifier. Average indoor humidity works just fine, but if the air's too dry, misting it once in a while will keep it looking its best.

4. Soil:

Well-draining soil is key. Think of it as giving your plant comfy shoes—nothing too tight, nothing too loose, but just right.

One of the best parts about the Song of India is how it grows. It's not going to take over your living room like some wild vine. It grows at a steady pace, rewarding your care with new, bright green and off white variegated leaves. And with a little trimming, you can keep it as a small, tidy plant, or let it stretch out into a tall, elegant beauty.

You'll also love how resilient this plant is. Forget to water it? No problem—it'll bounce back. Not enough light? It might grow a bit slower, but it'll still hang in there. This plant understands that life gets busy—it just asks for a bit of love when you can spare it.

This is a Plant That Never Fades. What makes the Song of India stand out among indoor plants is its ability to keep its striking appearance all year long. Its variegated leaves don't lose their vibrancy, even when the seasons change. Whether it's perched on your windowsill, brightening up your office, or nestled in a less-than-bright corner, it keeps the same elegant charm day in and day out.

So, for a beginner like you, the Song of India is a perfect choice. It brings a splash of tropical magic to your home while asking for little in return. It's the plant equivalent of a loyal friend—beautiful, reliable, and always there to brighten your day.

D. Pandan Grass

Pandan Grass is a low-maintenance plant that can handle a lot of sun, making it an excellent choice for beginners who might be worried about constant plant care. It's also a beautiful addition to your garden, with its long, green, blade-like leaves adding texture and a tropical feel. This tropical plant can also adapt to partial shade. Its tolerance to sun, combined with its minimal care requirements, makes it an ideal plant for outdoor gardens in warm climates.

If you're planting outdoors, choose a spot where the plant will get plenty of light throughout the day. Make sure the area has well-draining soil since Pandan Grass doesn't like waterlogged conditions.

For container gardening, select a pot with drainage holes and fill it with a mix of well-draining soil and organic matter to help it thrive.

You can start your Pandan Grass journey from either a cutting or a small seedling from a nursery. If you're lucky enough to get a cutting, make sure it has a healthy root system. Healthy roots look white.

Watering and Care

One of the best things about Pandan Grass is its tolerance to the sun, but it does appreciate regular watering. Aim to keep the soil consistently moist, especially during hot weather. However, avoid letting it sit in waterlogged soil. A good rule of thumb is to water when the top inch of soil feels dry.

Common Mistakes to Avoid

Pandan Grass is a forgiving plant, but there are a few common mistakes beginners should watch out for:

- **Overwatering:** This is probably the biggest issue for new plant owners. Pandan Grass doesn't like sitting in water, so always ensure the soil drains well.
- **Lack of Sunlight:** Although it can tolerate partial shade, Pandan Grass thrives in full sun. Make sure it's getting enough light to keep the leaves healthy and fragrant.
- **Ignoring Cold Temperatures:** Pandan Grass is a tropical plant and does not tolerate cold climates. If you're in a colder climate, bring the plant indoors or protect it during the winter.

Growing Pandan Grass is an enjoyable and rewarding experience, especially for beginners. It's a low-maintenance plant that brings both beauty and practicality to your home garden. With just a little sunlight, water, and care, you can have a healthy plant.

E. DEVILS BACKBONE

Meet the Devil's Backbone—a plant with a personality as intriguing as its name! Don't let the spooky title fool you, though. This hardy plant is more like a quirky friend than a troublemaker, perfect for beginners who want a resilient, sun-loving companion. With its distinctive zig-zagging stems and variegated leaves with pinkish tips, this plant is sure to grab attention. This sun-loving plant is easy to care for and an excellent choice for beginners. This plant thrives in full sunlight, making it perfect for those who have sunny spaces. Whether you're looking for a striking garden plant or a bold container feature, Devil's Backbone won't disappoint.

It's actually a low-maintenance plant that doesn't demand much attention—perfect for beginners who want to dip their toes into gardening without breaking a sweat. It's pretty chill when it comes to care.

Planting and Care

This sun-worshipping plant craves light. Whether it's indoors by a sun-filled window or outdoors basking in the rays, make sure your Devil's Backbone gets plenty of sunlight. It can handle partial shade, but for the best results, let it sunbathe. You'll notice its leaves becoming more vibrant when it's living its best sunny life.

And let's talk about soil. Devil's Backbone isn't picky, but it does appreciate well-draining soil. If planting in a pot, make sure there are drainage holes, and maybe throw in some cactus or succulent mix. Why? Because like a true rebel, this plant does not do soggy situations.

The plant's hardy nature means it doesn't need constant attention. Watering once a month in normal weather and twice a month in summers is best. When watering, allow the soil to dry out between sessions, as it's drought-tolerant and stores water in its thick stems. It's a succulent at heart and prefers things on the dry side. Too much water, and it might get dramatic, with its roots rotting. Not cool!

In hot climates, this plant handles the heat like a pro, but during cooler months or if temperatures drop, it's best to bring it indoors or keep it somewhere cozy.

Common Mistakes to Avoid

- **Overwatering**: Water once a month and this plant won't complain. In fact, if you don't water it, the leaves will simply go into hibernation mode with minimal leaves, thick stems, no growth but won't die on you. While it's tempting to be attentive, Devil's Backbone prefers dry spells between watering. Too much water can lead to root rot, so always check that the soil is dry before watering. In fact the only way to kill this plant is by overwatering.
- **Not Enough Sunlight**: This plant loves the sun! While it can survive in partial shade, it will truly thrive and grow its best in full sun. Legend has it that Devil's Backbone is named after its crooked, zigzagging stems that look like, well, a spine! It's the plant world's way of

standing out—literally. And if that's not enough to spark some garden envy, its leaves can turn red at the tips when exposed to lots of sunlight, adding a little extra flair to its already wild look.

- **Cold Weather**: Devil's Backbone isn't built for cold climates. If temperatures dip below 55°F (13°C), consider bringing it indoors or covering it to protect from the cold.

Toxicity Warning

As tough as it is, Devil's Backbone has a sap that can irritate the skin and is toxic to pets. It's best to keep this plant out of reach from pets and young children.

The Devil's Backbone is the kind of plant that thrives on neglect. Sun, a little water, and a laid-back attitude, and you've got yourself a winner. Whether you're a plant newbie or an experienced green thumb, this rebellious beauty will keep your garden looking lively without much hassle. Just remember: a little sunlight and space to shine, and the Devil's Backbone will do the rest.

Chapter 3
Mastering the Basics Without Breaking a Sweat

Now that you've chosen your first plants, let's dive into something even more exciting: keeping them happy and healthy! It might seem a bit intimidating at first, but don't worry—we've got you covered. Whether you're working with a hardy Snake Plant, a lush Money Plant, or even the gorgeous Song of India, understanding the fundamentals of plant care will ensure your green babies thrive under your loving watch.

So, grab a cup of tea (or coffee), settle into your favorite chair, and let's chat about the essentials—watering, light, soil, and avoiding some common beginner blunders!

Finding the Right Balance

Watering your plants isn't just a task—it's a conversation. Think of it like offering your plants a refreshing drink after a long day. But here's the catch: not every plant is as thirsty as the next. Some like to sip delicately, while others are ready to gulp down a whole glass. The trick? Learning their language.

- **Know Your Plant:** Picture this: your succulent is lounging in a desert, basking under the sun, and it could care less about the rain. Meanwhile, your tropical plant dreams of daily downpours. Getting to know your plant's natural habitat will tell you everything about how much water it craves. Think of it as finding out your new friend's favorite drink—hot or cold.
- **The Finger Test:** Forget fancy gadgets; you've got built-in plant sensors—your fingers! Just poke your finger about an inch into the soil. If it feels like you're touching the desert floor, it's time to water. If it's still slightly damp, your plant is probably still sipping on yesterday's drink.
- **Watering Frequency:** As a general rule, most houseplants are like weekend feasters—they're happy with a drink once a week. But don't be surprised if they ask for more in the summer

or go on a bit of a water diet in winter. Plants are pretty in tune with the seasons, after all.

- **Avoid Overwatering:** Overwatering is like offering someone a second slice of cake when they're already full—it's too much of a good thing. It leads to root rot, which is plant-speak for "I can't breathe!" Make sure your pots have drainage holes to let the extra water escape, like a tiny plant lifeboat.

LIGHT: FINDING THE PERFECT SPOT

Imagine your plant as a sunbather, always chasing the light. But just like we love different amounts of sunshine, so do our plants. The trick is finding that perfect spot where your plant can catch some rays without getting sunburned.

Understanding Light Levels:

- **Bright, Direct Light:** Think of this as your plant basking on a tropical beach—intense and warm. Plants like Aloe Vera and all succulents will thank you for placing them in the spotlight (literally).
- **Bright, Indirect Light:** This is more like lounging under a beach umbrella—plenty of

light, but not too harsh. Most houseplants love this middle ground. Imagine a room full of soft sunlight pouring in, but not directly hitting your leafy friends.

- **Low Light:** Think cozy and dim—perfect for reading a book, or, in the plant world, a spot for low-maintenance types like the snake and the ZZ plant. They won't complain about the lack of light; they'll just quietly keep growing.
- **Adjusting Light:** If your plant could wear sunglasses, it might be trying to tell you it's getting too much light. Scorched or bleached leaves? Too much sun! And if your plant looks like it's stretching for the stars (or the window), it's probably time to move it closer to some light.

Soil: The Foundation of Plant Health

Soil isn't just dirt; it's your plant's home. It's where they snuggle in, soak up nutrients, and put down roots—literally. So let's make sure we're setting them up in a place they love.

Choose the Right Soil:

- Potting Mix: Think of this as a mattress for most plants—a good potting mix offers just the right balance of softness and support, allowing your plants to rest comfortably while sipping on nutrients.
- If your succulent was human, it would probably enjoy lounging in a hammock on a sandy beach. Fast-draining, sandy soil is their happy place.
- Repotting: As your plant grows, it's going to need a bigger home. Think of it like upgrading from a starter apartment to a spacious condo. Fresh soil and a roomier pot will give your plant the freedom to stretch its roots and thrive.

COCOPEAT: A GREAT ALTERNATE TO SOIL

Coco peat is a superstar growing medium, perfect for beginners who want an easy, effective way to keep their plants healthy and happy. It's light, eco-friendly, and great at holding moisture without drowning your roots. Whether you're planting indoors, outdoors, or experimenting with container gardening, coco peat is a fantastic choice to make your gardening life easier.

Coco peat is incredibly sustainable! The process of making it includes using waste from the coconut industry, so not only are you giving your plants a great home, but you're also contributing to reducing agricultural waste. Talk about a win-win!

If plants had a preference for their bedding, coco peat would probably be at the top of the list. Think of it as the plant world's version of a memory foam mattress—light, breathable, and just the right amount of moisture. For those just starting their plant-growing journey, or even seasoned gardeners looking for a hassle-free medium, coco peat is your new best friend.

Why Use Coco Peat?

Coco peat is like the Goldilocks of growing mediums. It holds water, but not too much, and provides just the right balance of aeration for your plant's roots. This makes it ideal for beginners who might be a bit heavy-handed with the watering can. It acts as a buffer, giving your plants a stable environment without drowning their roots.

One of the best features of Coco peat is its moisture-retention capacity. It holds up to 10 times its weight in water, meaning your plants stay hydrated for longer stretches without you needing to water constantly. At the same time, excess water drains out easily, which prevents root rot—a common beginner mistake.

How to Use Coco Peat

Coco peat usually comes in compact blocks. You just need to add water, and voilà, it fluffs up like magic! Here's how you get it ready for planting:

1. **Break up the Block**: Coco peat often comes compressed, so break it into chunks.
2. **Add Water**: Slowly pour water over the chunks, and you'll see them expand before your eyes. Fluff it up with your hands until it's soft and crumbly.
3. **Mix with Other Mediums**: On its own, Coco peat can be a little too light for some plants. Many gardeners mix it with

compost, garden soil, or perlite to give it some extra heft and nutrients.

Why Plants Love Coco Peat

- **Excellent Drainage**: Coco peat ensures your plants never have soggy feet. Water drains well, yet the medium stays damp enough to nourish your plant's roots.
- **Great for Root Growth**: The texture of Coco peat provides plenty of space for roots to breathe, grow, and thrive without suffocating.
- **pH Neutral**: This medium is naturally pH neutral, meaning it won't affect your plant's acidity levels. It creates a balanced environment, ideal for a wide range of plants.
- **Pest-Free:** Since it's made from coconut husks, Coco peat doesn't attract pests or diseases. That's a huge relief for anyone who's faced a bug invasion!

Common Mistakes to Avoid

- **Not Mixing in Nutrients**: Coco peat on its own doesn't have a lot of nutrients, so you'll need to mix it with compost or regularly fertilize your plants to keep them happy.

- **Over-Watering:** While Coco peat holds water well, beginners might think it needs more water than it does. Actually, the thumb rule is that the watering needs in a Coco peat soil mix are reduced by half. If you water weekly in a soil pot, you should water every 2 weeks. Always check if the top inch is dry before reaching for the watering can again.

Common Beginner Mistakes (And How to Dodge Them Like a Pro)

Every new plant parent has a learning curve. But with a few tips, you'll avoid the most common pitfalls. Think of these as the "plant care pro tips" you didn't know you needed!

- **Overwatering:** Yes, we're back to this one. It's so easy to overdo it when you're trying to show your plants love. Remember, plants don't need a flood to feel the love—a gentle sprinkle will do. Always check the soil before watering.

- **Neglecting Light Needs:** Imagine putting a sun-loving plant in a dark room—it's not going to end well. Be mindful of light levels and give your plant the sun (or shade) it's craving.
- **Using the Wrong Soil:** Don't treat all soil the same. It's like trying to run a marathon in the wrong shoes—it won't end well. Get the right soil for your plant, and it'll reward you with strong, healthy growth.
- **Ignoring Signs of Stress:** Your plant isn't being dramatic when its leaves turn yellow or droop—it's sending you a message! Listen closely, adjust its care, and watch your plant perk up like magic.

And there you have it! With these basics, you're well on your way to creating a vibrant, green sanctuary. Remember, every plant has its personality and quirks, just like us. And as you get to know them better, you'll start feeling like a true plant whisperer—trust me, your plants will thank you.

Chapter 4

"Your First Plant Sanctuary"

Turning Corners into Green Retreats

Now that you've got the basics down, let's take it one step further and create a space where your plants can truly thrive. Think of it as building a little sanctuary, a peaceful retreat for both you and your leafy adventurous companions. Whether you've got a sunny windowsill, a cozy balcony, or even just a quiet corner in your room, you can transform it into a vibrant green haven that radiates joy and tranquility. And the best part? This is your chance to get creative and make it truly yours.

The first step in building your green haven is choosing a location that suits your plants' needs. This is like picking the perfect seat in a café—where does the light hit just right? For most houseplants, a spot near a bright window will do wonders. A sunny windowsill is practically plant paradise.

If space is tight, don't worry! You can still work some plant magic. Think vertically—shelves, plant stands, or even hanging planters can maximize your space. It's like giving your plants a penthouse view!

Now comes the fun part—arranging your plants! Think of it as curating your own little jungle. Taller plants can stand proudly in the back, while shorter ones can take the spotlight up front. This creates a layered look that adds depth and visual interest. Plus, it just feels like your plants are hanging out together, each one adding its unique flair to the group.

To make things easier on yourself, group plants with similar light and water needs together. That way, you won't be running around, trying to remember which plant needs what. It's like building a little plant family, where everyone thrives together.

Your green space isn't just for your plants—it's for you, too! So, why not let it reflect your personality and style? Whether you prefer minimalist vibes or something more eclectic, there's no right or wrong here. Consider choosing decorative pots that catch your eye, adding colorful plant stands, or even placing some artwork nearby that complements your plants. These little touches can turn your green retreat into something that feels uniquely you.

Want to take it up a notch? Add small elements like pebbles, moss, or tiny statues around your plants. These little details can elevate your space and make it feel like a mini garden escape.

And there you have it! You've laid the foundation, not just for growing your healthy plants family, but for creating a space that brings joy to your home. As you continue on this journey, remember that your green haven is more than just a collection of plants. It's a living, breathing part of your life, and as you grow, so will your plants.

You're no longer just a beginner—you're now stepping into the world of an intermediate plant lover. So take a deep breath, admire your work, and get ready for the next chapter of this adventure. The journey has only just begun.

This wraps up Section 1 of your plant journey. You've learned the basics, created your green space, and are now well-equipped to grow not just plants but your passion for this incredible hobby. Ready for more? Let's move on to the next phase—where the real magic begins!

SECTION 2: GROWING WITH CONFIDENCE (INTERMEDIATE)

Chapter 5

Building Your Plant Family

Congratulations on mastering the basics! Now that you've got the hang of plant care, it's time to dive into expanding your green paradise. Adding new plants not only enhances the beauty of your space but also deepens your connection with the plant world.

In this chapter, we'll explore 15 indoor and shade-loving plants, and 15 sun-loving plants to broaden your collection. Let's get started!

Indoor and Shade-Loving Plants

5 Flowering or Colored Foliage Plants:

1. **Peace Lily:** The Peace Lily is a stunning plant with glossy, dark green leaves and elegant red and white blooms that resemble a hooded shape. It thrives in low to medium indirect light, making it perfect for spots like living rooms or bedrooms where sunlight is filtered.

Peace Lilies prefer well-draining soil and need to be watered when the top inch of soil feels dry—avoid overwatering, as they don't like soggy roots. Placing them in a bright, shady corner will help them flourish, adding a touch of tranquility to your space.

2. **Begonia:** Begonias are vibrant plants known for their colorful leaves and delicate blooms, which range from reds and pinks to yellows and whites. They thrive in bright, indirect light, making them ideal for a spot near a window with filtered sunlight. Begonias prefer well-draining soil that's kept slightly moist but not soggy. Water them when the top inch of soil is dry. A cozy corner in your living room or kitchen is perfect for these beauties, as they enjoy humidity. With the right care, Begonias can bring a cheerful splash of color to any indoor space.
3. **Aglonema:** Aglonema, often called Chinese Evergreen, is a beautiful plant with broad, glossy leaves that come in shades of green, silver, and sometimes red. It's a hardy plant that thrives in low to medium indirect light, making it perfect for dimmer areas like offices or bedrooms. Aglonema prefers well-draining

soil and should be watered when the top inch of soil feels dry—avoid overwatering to prevent root rot. It's a low-maintenance plant, ideal for a cozy corner with moderate light. With its striking foliage, Aglonema adds a touch of elegance to any indoor space.

4. **Croton:** Crotons are eye-catching plants known for their bold, colorful leaves, which display a mix of reds, yellows, oranges, and greens. These vibrant plants love bright, indirect light, making them perfect for a sunny spot near a window. Crotons prefer well-draining soil and need to be watered when the top inch of soil feels dry. The key is to keep the soil evenly moist but not soggy. They thrive in warm, humid environments, so placing them in a bright bathroom or a sunlit living room is ideal. With their striking foliage, Crotons add a splash of color and tropical flair to your home.
5. **Syngonium:** Syngonium, also known as Arrowhead Plant, is a lovely houseplant with arrow-shaped leaves that start green and can develop shades of white, pink, or even cream as they mature. It thrives in low to medium indirect light, making it a great choice for a

shady corner or an office desk. Syngonium prefers well-draining soil and should be watered when the top inch of soil feels dry—it's best to keep the soil consistently moist but not waterlogged. With its compact growth and easy care, Syngonium is perfect for adding a touch of greenery to any indoor space.

5 Non-Flowering Indoor Plants:

1. **Areca Palm:** The Areca Palm, also known as the Butterfly Palm, is a stunning plant that instantly brings a tropical feel to any room. With its soft, feathery fronds that gracefully arch out, it's like having a piece of paradise indoors. This plant thrives in bright, indirect light, making it ideal for a sunny living room or near a window. Areca palms love well-draining soil and should be watered when the top inch feels dry—just enough to keep the soil slightly moist. Imagine this elegant palm transforming your space into a lush, green oasis—it's the perfect way to add natural beauty and serenity to your home.
2. **Cast Iron Plant:** The Cast Iron Plant is a true gem for any plant lover, boasting lush, dark

green, and glossy leaves that bring a touch of elegance to your space. As its name suggests—it's incredibly tough and resilient, thriving in low to bright, indirect light. This makes it perfect for those dim corners or north-facing rooms where other plants might struggle. Cast Iron Plants prefer well-draining soil and should be watered when the top inch feels dry—just enough to keep it happy without overwatering. Imagine this hardy beauty effortlessly brightening up your home with its sleek foliage; it's a low-maintenance plant that's both striking and forgiving.

3. **Dracaena:** The Dracaena plant is a standout with its striking, sword-like leaves that come in shades of green, red, and even variegated patterns. It's a real showstopper, adding a touch of drama and sophistication to any room. Dracaenas thrive in bright, indirect light, making them perfect for a sunny spot or near a window. They prefer well-draining soil and should be watered when the top inch of soil feels dry—keeping it moist but not soggy. With its sleek, architectural foliage, the Dracaena is an easy-care beauty that effortlessly elevates your space, making it a

tempting choice for anyone looking to add a touch of elegance to their home.

4. **Fiddle Leaf Fig:** The Fiddle Leaf Fig is an absolute showstopper with its large, glossy, fiddle-shaped leaves that instantly command attention. Its bold foliage adds a dramatic touch to any space, making it a must-have for a stylish, modern home. This plant loves bright, indirect light, so it's perfect for a sunny corner or near a window with filtered sunlight. It prefers well-draining soil and should be watered when the top inch feels dry—be cautious not to overwater, as it doesn't like soggy roots. Imagine the Fiddle Leaf Fig as the striking centerpiece of your room, effortlessly bringing elegance and a fresh, vibrant vibe to your home.
5. **Raphis Palm:** Rhapis Palm, is a stunning hardy plant with fan-shaped leaves and elegant clustered stems that bring a touch of sophistication to any room. Its lush, green fronds add a refined, tropical charm, making it a perfect centrepiece for stylish interiors. Thriving in bright, indirect light, the Fan Raphis is ideal for a well-lit corner or near a window with filtered sunlight. It prefers

well-draining soil and should be watered when the top inch feels dry. Raphis Palm would add grace to your home with its foliage, effortlessly adding a touch of elegance and tranquility to your space.

5 Indoor Creepers:

1. **String of Pearls:** The String of Pearls is a mesmerizing succulent with its unique, bead-like leaves that cascade beautifully in long, trailing strands. Its distinctive, round pearls add a playful and charming touch to any space, making it a standout choice for hanging baskets or high shelves. This plant loves bright, indirect light, so it's perfect for a sunny spot with filtered sunlight. It prefers well-draining soil and should be watered sparingly—let the soil dry out completely between waterings. Imagine this exotic beauty draping gracefully from a hanging pot, adding a touch of whimsy and elegance to your home with its enchanting, pearl-like foliage.
2. **English Ivy:** English Ivy is a captivating plant with its lush, trailing vines and glossy, heart-shaped leaves with 3 edges that add a touch of classic charm to any space. Its

vigorous growth and versatile nature make it perfect for cascading from hanging baskets or climbing up trellises. Thriving in bright, indirect light, English Ivy is ideal for spots near a window with filtered sunlight. It prefers well-draining soil. Keep the soil consistently moist and trim the vines regularly to keep it under control.

3. **Philodendron Cordatum:** The Philodendron Cordatum, also known as the Heartleaf Philodendron, is a stunning plant with its lush, heart-shaped leaves that cascade gracefully from trailing vines. Its vibrant green foliage adds a touch of lush elegance to any space, making it perfect for hanging baskets or as a tabletop accent. Thriving in low to bright, indirect light, it's a versatile choice for various spots in your home. The Philodendron Cordatum prefers well-draining soil and should be watered when the top inch of soil feels dry. Picture the Philodendron Cordatum adding a splash of vibrant greenery and effortless charm to your space, creating a refreshing, inviting atmosphere.
4. **Curtain Creeper:** The Curtain Creeper is a stunning plant with its cascading vines and

delicate, heart-shaped leaves that create a lush, green curtain of foliage. Its vibrant growth makes it perfect for draping over trellises or hanging baskets, adding a touch of natural beauty and elegance to any space. Thriving in bright, indirect light, it's ideal for a sunny spot with filtered sunlight. This plant prefers well-draining soil and should be watered when the top inch feels dry—keeping it consistently moist but not soggy. Imagine the Curtain Creeper enhancing your decor with its graceful, verdant trails, effortlessly bringing a refreshing, tropical vibe to your home.

5. **Maidenhair Vine:** The Maidenhair Vine is like a delicate lacework of greenery, perfect for those who love a touch of elegance in their garden. With its fine, wiry stems and tiny round leaves, it's a graceful creeper that does well in shaded spots, whether indoors or outdoors. This plant is a great choice for hanging baskets or letting it trail along a shelf, bringing a soft, natural charm to any space.

When it comes to care, the Maidenhair Vine is fairly low-maintenance. It prefers indirect light or partial shade, making it ideal for those tricky spots that don't get a lot of sun. The key to keeping this beauty happy is well-draining soil. Water it regularly, but don't let it sit in soggy soil—just ensure the top inch dries out between waterings. During the growing season, i.e., summer, feeding it with vermicompost every few weeks will help it stay lush and healthy.

One thing to watch out for: it can be a bit of a wanderer! Trim it back if it starts getting too wild, and enjoy its graceful presence in your home or garden. The Maidenhair Vine is a delightful creeper that adds life to any shaded corner.

We've just explored 15 fantastic indoor plants—5 with vibrant, colorful foliage, 5 that bring lush greenery indoors, and 5 beautiful creepers. Each one adds its own unique charm to your space. Now that you're ready to fill your home with these green companions, it's time to step outside!

In the next section, we'll dive into 15 sun-loving plants that thrive outdoors. Get ready to soak up some sunlight and discover new favorites for your garden!"

15 Sun-Loving Plants

5 Flowering Plants:

1. **Hibiscus:** The Hibiscus is a dazzling plant known for its large, vibrant flowers that come in shades of red, pink, orange, and yellow. Each bloom is like a tropical sunset, adding a burst of color and cheer to your garden or home. It thrives in bright, direct light, making it perfect for a sunny window or garden spot. Hibiscus plants love well-draining soil and should be watered regularly, keeping the soil consistently moist but not waterlogged. For best results, use a vermicompost every 4-6 weeks during the growing season to encourage lush blooms and healthy growth. Hibiscus with its eye-catching, colorful flowers, would definitely bring a touch of tropical paradise right to your doorstep.
2. **Rose:** Roses are the epitome of floral elegance, boasting velvety petals in an array of colors from deep reds to soft pinks and sunny yellows. Their classic, fragrant blooms create a

stunning display that captivates any garden or indoor space. Roses thrive in bright, direct light, so place them in a sunny spot where they can soak up the sun. They prefer well-draining soil enriched with organic matter, and watering should be done deeply but infrequently, allowing the soil to dry out between waterings. To keep them blooming beautifully, use a vermicompost every 4-6 weeks during the growing season. Prune the stem right after the flower is dried. These timeless beauties with their vibrant colors and delightful scent will turn your garden into a floral paradise.

3. **Vinca:** Vinca, also known as Periwinkle, is a charming plant with its vibrant flowers that bloom in a range of colors, from vivid purples to soft pinks and bright whites. Its glossy green leaves complement the colorful blooms, creating a lively, eye-catching display. Vinca thrives in bright, direct light, so it's perfect for sun-drenched spots in your garden or on a windowsill. It prefers well-draining soil and should be watered regularly. Use a Vermicompost every 4-6 weeks. Vinca will add a splash of color and cheer to your space,

effortlessly brightening up your garden or home with its stunning, vibrant flowers.

4. **Jasmine:** Jasmine is renowned for its delicate, star-shaped flowers that emit a sweet, unforgettable fragrance. Blooming in shades of white, these lovely flowers add a touch of elegance and charm to any garden. Jasmine thrives in bright, direct light, making it perfect for a sunny spot where it can bask in the warmth. It prefers well-draining soil and should be watered regularly. Use vermicompost every 4-6 weeks. Jasmine's scent and beautiful blooms will transform your space into a fragrant, and delightful atmosphere.
5. **Lantana:** Lantana is a vibrant, show-stopping plant with clusters of colorful flowers that light up your garden with fiery oranges, radiant reds, and cheerful yellows. These cheerful blooms create a lively, eye-catching effect. Lantanas thrive in bright, direct sunlight, making them perfect for sunny spots. They prefer well-draining soil and are quite drought-tolerant, so you don't need to water them frequently. To keep them blooming abundantly, vermicompost every 6-8 weeks

during the growing season. Lantanas can create a bed of flowers in summers.

5 Non-Flowering Plants:

1. **Tulsi:** Tulsi, or Holy Basil, is a captivating plant with its rich green leaves and charming purple blooms that offer both beauty and serenity. Found in almost every Indian household, revered in many cultures for its spiritual and healing properties, Tulsi thrives in bright, direct sunlight. It loves well-draining soil and should be watered regularly. Tulsi is not just a plant; it's a touch of tranquility and a symbol of vitality in your home.
2. **Aloe Vera:** This succulent loves full sun and dry conditions. Water thoroughly and let the soil dry out completely between waterings. It's also great for soothing minor burns.
3. **Jade Plant:** Jade Plants prefer full sun and well-drained soil. Water thoroughly and let the soil dry out between waterings. It's a hardy succulent that can grow quite large.
4. **Agave:** Agave is a stunning sun-loving plant that embodies resilience and beauty. Known for its striking rosette shape and thick, fleshy

leaves, Agave thrives in full sunlight, making it a perfect addition to gardens and landscapes in warm climates. Agave is incredibly drought-tolerant, requiring minimal water once established, which makes it an excellent choice for low-maintenance gardening. Its sharp, pointed leaves add a dramatic flair, while its ability to adapt to poor soil conditions means it can flourish in rocky or sandy areas. Agave not only enhances your garden's aesthetic but also offers a striking contrast to softer plants, creating a stunning visual impact in any sun-drenched spot. With little care beyond occasional watering, this hardy succulent is sure to thrive and impress.

5. **Cactus:** Cacti are the ultimate sun-loving plants, perfectly designed to thrive in bright, arid environments. With their unique shapes and stunning variety, cacti bring a touch of the desert to your garden or home. These hardy succulents are masters of water conservation, storing moisture in their thick, fleshy stems, allowing them to flourish with minimal care. They thrive in full sunlight, soaking up those rays and adding vibrant textures and colors to your space. Cacti come adorned with spines or

soft fuzz, which not only add character but also help protect them from herbivores and reduce water loss. Ideal for low-maintenance gardens, these plants are perfect for anyone looking to add a bit of drama without the hassle of watering. With just a little love and occasional watering—maybe once a quarter, Cacti can turn any sunny spot into a striking oasis, showcasing nature's artistry and resilience in a delightful way.

5 Sun-Loving Creepers

1. **The Blue Star Creeper:** The Blue Star Creeper is a delightful, sun-loving plant that's perfect for brightening up any sunny spot. With its tiny, star-shaped blue flowers and lush, green foliage, it creates a charming, carpet-like effect that adds a splash of color to your garden or containers. This hardy plant thrives in full sun and loves well-draining soil. It's low-maintenance and only needs occasional watering.
2. **Bougainvillea:** Bougainvillea is a dazzling creeper that thrives in full sun, making it a perfect choice for bright, sunny spots. Its vibrant, papery bracts come in shades of

bright pink, light pink, red, and orange, creating a breathtaking display that can transform any space into a tropical paradise. Bougainvillea loves well-draining soil and seldom needs watering. It's a stunning, low-maintenance plant that effortlessly brightens up your outdoor space.

3. **Sweet Potato Vine:** The Sweet Potato Creeper is a fantastic sun-loving plant that's as charming as it is versatile. With its heart-shaped leaves and vibrant foliage, it creates a lush, cascading effect that's perfect for adding a touch of greenery to sunny spots. It thrives in full sun and well-draining soil, and is remarkably low-maintenance. It provides a beautiful, colorful cover and a burst of natural beauty in the sunniest corners of your outdoor space.
4. **Yellow Mandevilla:** The Yellow Mandevilla Creeper is a showstopper that thrives in full sun, making it a brilliant choice for bright, sunny spots. Its vibrant yellow flowers, with their trumpet-like shape and glossy green leaves, create a stunning, tropical effect that instantly elevates your space. This plant loves well-draining soil and should be watered

regularly. It's a low-maintenance beauty that effortlessly brings a touch of exotic charm to any sunny spot.

5. **Orange Trumpet Vine:** The Orange Trumpet Vine is a dazzling sun-loving creeper that brings a burst of vibrant color to any sunny spot. With its striking, trumpet-shaped orange flowers and lush green foliage, it creates a stunning, cascading effect that adds a touch of tropical flair to your garden. This hardy plant thrives in full sun and well-draining soil. This vine can drape over your garden, its blooms creating a vivid, eye-catching lively display.

Congratulations! You've just met 15 fabulous indoor plants and 15 sun-loving stars—now you're ready to bring these leafy friends home. Whether your living room needs a green upgrade or your sunlit balcony could use some plant love, you've got the perfect options to choose from.

With this new knowledge, you're all set to create your very own plant paradise. Just remember, once you start talking to your plants (trust me, it happens!), don't be surprised if they seem to thrive even more. Happy planting!

Chapter 6

When Things Go Wrong

"And How to Fix Them Like a Pro"

As your collection grows, so does the complexity of caring for different species. Each plant has its own requirements for light, water, and nutrients.

Here's how to keep your diverse collection thriving:

- **Light:** Different plants have varying light needs. For example, Snake Plant and ZZ thrive in low to medium light, while succulents and cacti need bright, direct light. Group your plants accordingly to ensure they receive the appropriate amount of light.
- **Water:** As you add more plants to your collection, you'll need to pay closer

attention to their individual watering needs. Some plants prefer consistently moist soil, while others, like succulents, need their soil to dry out completely between waterings.

- **Humidity:** Many tropical plants, such as Money Plant and ZZ thrive in high humidity. Consider using a humidifier or placing a tray of water near your plants to increase the humidity in the room. Alternatively, grouping plants together can also help create a more humid microenvironment.
- **Feeding:** As plants grow, they need nutrients to stay healthy. Use a balanced, vermicompost during the growing season (spring and summer) to provide essential nutrients. Be careful not to over-fertilize, as this can cause nutrient burn and damage your plants.

Despite all care and precautions, you'll inevitably face some challenges. But don't worry! Every plant lover encounters issues, and with a bit of knowledge, you can handle them like a pro. Let's dive into some common plant challenges and how to overcome them.

Pests and Diseases

1. **Aphids:** These tiny insects suck sap from plants, leading to curled or yellowing leaves. Use insecticidal soap or a mixture of water and dish soap to get rid of them. Regularly check your plants for signs of these pests.

2. **Spider Mites:** These pests cause stippling or tiny spots on leaves. Increase humidity around your plants and wash them with a strong stream of water to dislodge these mites.

3. **Mealybugs:** These white, cottony pests can be found in leaf joints and on stems. Remove them with a cotton swab dipped in diluted alcohol, and treat the plant with insecticidal soap if needed.

4. **Fungus Gnats:** These tiny flying insects are usually a sign of overwatering. Allow the soil to dry out between waterings and use sticky traps to catch the adults.

5. Powdery Mildew: This white, powdery fungus often appears in humid conditions. Improve air circulation around your plants.

If you notice your plant is heavily infected with any of these, the best thing is to cut the branch off the main plant. This will prevent the sick plant from dying and help it revive faster.

DISEASES: PREVENTION AND TREATMENT

Plant diseases can be tricky to diagnose and treat, but early detection is key to keeping your plants healthy. Here are some common plant diseases and how to manage them:

1. **Powdery Mildew:** This fungal disease appears as a white, powdery substance on leaves. It thrives in warm, dry conditions with poor air circulation. To prevent powdery mildew, increase air circulation around your plants and avoid overhead watering. The best natural treatment is washing the shoots with garlic crushed water, soapy water and yes, after treating the plant with both of these, remember

to give them a shower in 24 hours. Within 2-3 days, you will see your plant smiling back at you.

2. **Root Rot:** Overwatering is the main cause of root rot, a fungal disease that causes roots to become mushy and black. To prevent root rot, ensure your pots have proper drainage, and avoid letting plants sit in water. If root rot occurs, remove the affected roots and repot the plant in fresh, well-draining soil.
3. **Leaf Spot:** This bacterial or fungal disease causes dark, water-soaked spots on leaves. It spreads in wet, humid conditions. Remove affected leaves and improve air circulation around the plant. Avoid overhead watering and treat with a fungicide if needed.

Pruning: Encouraging Healthy Growth

Pruning is an essential part of plant care. It helps shape the plant, remove dead or damaged leaves, and encourage new growth. Here's how to prune your plants effectively:

1. **Deadheading:** For flowering plants, remove spent blooms to encourage the plant to produce more flowers. This process is called Deadheading and keeps the plant looking tidy.
2. **Removing Dead or Damaged Leaves:** Regularly remove any yellowing, dead, or damaged leaves to prevent disease and improve the plant's appearance.
3. **Shaping:** Pruning can also help shape your plant, controlling its size and encouraging bushier growth. Use clean, sharp scissors or pruning shears to trim back stems just above a leaf node (the point where a leaf attaches to the stem).

Repotting: Giving Your Plants Room to Grow

As your plants grow, they may outgrow their pots. Repotting gives the roots more room to expand and provides the plant with fresh soil and nutrients.

When to Repot: Signs that your plant needs repotting include roots growing out of the drainage holes, water sitting on the surface of the soil without being absorbed, or the plant becoming top-heavy and falling over.

How to Repot: Choose a pot that is one size larger than the current pot, with drainage holes at the bottom. Gently remove the plant from its current pot, shake off the old soil, and trim any dead or damaged roots. Place the plant in the new pot, fill it with fresh soil, and water thoroughly.

Propagating: Growing new plants from cuttings is a rewarding way to expand your collection. For most plants, take a healthy cutting, remove the lower leaves, and place it in water or soil until roots develop.

With these tips, you're well-equipped to handle the common challenges that come with plant care. Remember, every problem has a solution, and each challenge is an opportunity to learn and grow as a plant lover.

Ready to continue your journey? With your expanding collection and newfound knowledge, you're well on your way to mastering the art of plant care. Onward to new green adventures!

Chapter 7

Designing a Plant-Filled Home

Your plant collection has grown, and now it's time to showcase your leafy friends in style. Designing a plant-filled home isn't just about placing plants in corners; it's about creating spaces that are both visually appealing and functional. Let's explore how to create stunning plant displays that will make your home feel like a lush oasis.

- **The Power of Grouping:** Grouping plants together can create a more dynamic and visually interesting display. Try combining plants of different heights, textures, and colors. Place taller plants in the back and shorter ones in front for a layered effect.
- **Color Coordination:** Think about how the colors of your plants and their pots

work together. A mix of green tones with vibrant flowering plants can make a stunning impact.

- **Vertical Space:** Utilize vertical space by adding shelves or plant stands. This not only saves floor space but also adds dimension to your plant display. Arrange plants at varying heights to create visual interest.
- **Tiered Stands:** Consider using tiered plant stands or ladders to display multiple plants in one spot. This is a great way to showcase trailing plants and create a cascading effect.
- **Wall Gardens:** Create a vertical garden or plant wall by mounting planters or using hanging pockets. This is a fantastic way to bring greenery to blank walls and add a touch of nature indoors.
- **Hanging Planters:** Use hangers or stylish hanging pots to display plants at eye level. Hanging plants can add a unique element to any room and make use of overhead space.

Balancing Plant Care with Décor:

- **Functional Décor:** Choose decorative pots and planters that complement your home's style. Consider materials like ceramic, terracotta, bamboo or woven baskets that fit your décor while being practical for plant care.
- **Mix and Match:** Mix plants with other home décor elements like candles, books, or sculptures. This can help integrate plants into your overall home design and make them feel like a natural part of the space.

Creating a Cohesive Look

- **Color Themes:** Coordinate plants with a specific color theme to create a cohesive look. For instance, a collection of plants with silvery or blue-toned leaves can give a calming, cohesive appearance.
- **Style Themes:** Choose a style that reflects your personal taste—whether it's boho chic with hangers and trailing plants or a minimalist look with sleek planters and simple foliage.

Practical Considerations:

- **Light and Accessibility:** Ensure that your plant displays are practical. Place plants in locations where they receive the appropriate light and are easily accessible for watering and care.
- **Temperature and Humidity:** Consider the temperature and humidity needs of your plants when arranging them. Group plants with similar needs together to make care easier.

Chapter 8

Train Your Plants to Live When you are Away

You have become a devoted plant parent, nurturing your leafy little family can feel like running a botanical daycare. You've painstakingly curated a collection of greens, each one a unique character in your home jungle.

But then, reality strikes: the thought of leaving them behind for a weekend getaway fills you with dread. Who will water your precious plants while you're gone? Your neighbor might mistakenly think the Snake Plant is thirsty and drown it in love, while your well-meaning friend could confuse your succulent(s) for a very needy dog. Will they remember that your beloved ZZ Plant is more of a 'less-is-more' kind of drinker? It's like leaving your kids with a babysitter—except these kids are rooted to the spot and depend on you for their survival. The mental images of your poor, neglected plants wilting away while you're lounging on the beach are enough to send you into a spiral of guilt. So, while you're dreaming of sun-soaked shores, your heart is stuck in a tug-of-war between plant love and wanderlust. Will they wither away in your absence? After all, plants can't exactly text you if they need a drink of water!

Ah, the trials of being a plant parent.

Well, you're not alone in this worry. Every plant lover has felt this anxiety, but here's the good news: with a little preparation, you can train your plants to fend for themselves for a couple of weeks. Yes, you can enjoy your holiday guilt-free, knowing your green friends will be just fine.

Let's dive into a few easy, low-cost methods to ensure your green friends stay hydrated and happy while you're away.

Start by Knowing Your Plants' Needs

First things first, get to know your plants' watering needs. Some plants, like succulents or snake plants, are perfectly happy with infrequent watering. Others, like ferns or herbs, tend to throw a fit if they don't get their regular drink. But no matter your plant type, with a few clever techniques, you can set them up to survive—and even thrive—while you're away.

Now, let's dive into some tried-and-tested methods that make sure your plants stay hydrated and happy while you're off living your best life.

The Drip Irrigation Method

Drip irrigation is one of the easiest and most effective ways to ensure your plants get a steady supply of water. And the best part? You don't need any fancy equipment.

Here's what you'll need:

- A plastic bottle with a cap
- A needle or pin
- A steady hand (don't worry, it's simpler than it sounds!)

To set this up, fill the plastic bottle with water and poke a few tiny holes in the cap with a needle. The smaller the holes, the slower the water will drip out, giving your plants a consistent supply of moisture. Next, bury the bottle neck-deep into the soil of your potted plant or garden bed. That's it! The bottle will slowly release water into the soil as needed, keeping your plants perfectly hydrated while you sip mojitos on the beach.

If you have bigger plants or a lot of thirsty greens, consider using multiple bottles and bigger ones – the 2 liters Coke/Pepsi or Bisleri kind.

This method is especially great for outdoor as well as indoor plants. It's like having a personal plant sitter—only quieter!

Capillary Action: The Slow and Steady Irrigator

Capillary action-based irrigation might sound complicated, but it's surprisingly simple. This method relies on the natural ability of water to move through materials like cloth.

Here's what you'll need:

- A large source of water – bucket full/drum

- Strips of cotton cloth (old T-shirt, any cotton clothes or thick string of Jute or Cotton (natural fibres work best)
- A little bit of patience

Place the bucket close to your plants, and drape one end of the cotton string into the water. The other end should rest 2-3 inches deep into the soil. And voila! The magic of capillary action begins. The rope will draw water from the bowl and deliver it to your plant's roots slowly and steadily, just like a friend who remembers to text you "Hey, how are you?" every once in a while.

This hack works wonders for plants. It's low-tech, but it works like magic!

Mulching: The Secret Weapon

Here's a hack that often flies under the radar: mulching. It's not just for outdoor gardens; your indoor plants will appreciate it too. By covering the surface of the soil with a layer of mulch (this could be wood chips, pebbles, or even waste paper), you can help lock in moisture and reduce evaporation.

Think of it as a cozy blanket for your plants' roots. While you're off exploring, they'll stay snug and hydrated under their protective cover, even if the room gets a little warm or dry.

The High-Tech Drip Irrigation with Timers

For the gadget lovers out there, technology has some brilliant solutions. There are automated drip-irrigation tools which can be connected directly to tap and the whole system is either switch-based or can even connect to your smartphone, allowing you to monitor and water your plants remotely. Imagine checking in on your plants from across the world and making sure they get a little sip of water when needed. We truly live in the future!

You've Got This!

Now that you've mastered the art of training your plants to survive while you're away, you can book that vacation without a second thought.

The key takeaway here is this: your plants are stronger and more adaptable than you think. With a little preparation, they'll flourish without you for a few weeks, and you'll come back to a house full of happy, healthy plants. And who knows? They might even surprise you by growing a little taller, showing off a new leaf, or blooming while you're gone.

Chapter 9

The Joy of Sharing

Plants have a magical way of bringing people together. There's something deeply satisfying about nurturing a tiny sprout into a full-grown plant and then sharing that joy with others. Whether you're trading cuttings with a friend, gifting a plant to a loved one, or joining a community of fellow plant lovers, the act of sharing your green thumb creates bonds that last. Let's dive into how sharing your plants can enrich both your life and the lives of those around you.

Plants as Gifts with Meaning

A Living Gift: Gifting someone a plant is more than just handing over a pot of greenery—it's offering them a living companion. Plants grow and evolve over time, serving as a constant reminder of the connection you share. Every new leaf is a small celebration of growth, both for the plant and the person caring for it.

Symbolism and Thoughtfulness: Think about the person you're gifting the plant to—do they need a little cheer in their life? A bright, flowering plant like a Peace Lily can lift up their spirits. Or perhaps they need something resilient, like a ZZ Plant, to remind them of their own inner strength. The thought you put into the plant's symbolism adds a layer of meaning to your gift.

And remember to add a sticker of care on the pot before gifting—a new plant parent would definitely need it.

PASSING DOWN GREEN TRADITIONS

Family Heirlooms: Some plants have stories behind them, passed down from generation to generation. Imagine sharing a cutting from a plant your grandmother nurtured, continuing a living tradition. Each new home that plant enters carries a piece of the past with it.

Creating New Traditions: Even if your plant doesn't have a history, you can start a new tradition. Gift your siblings, friends, colleagues, guests, children or grandchildren plants to care for, teaching them the joys and responsibilities of plant care. This can foster a lifelong connection to nature and a deeper understanding of the cycle of life.

The Simple Joy of Plant Swaps

Exchanging Knowledge and Greenery: Imagine a group of friends gathering in a cozy backyard, each with a cutting or small plant to share. A plant swap is not just about exchanging plants; it's about exchanging stories, tips, and enthusiasm. You may leave with a new plant, but the real treasure is the connection you've made with fellow plant lovers.

Cultivating Friendships: When you give someone a cutting from your favorite plant, you're sharing a piece of your home. As they nurture that cutting into a new plant, they'll think of you. These simple exchanges can grow into friendships, rooted in a shared love for nature.

The Strength of the Plant Community

A Space to Share Your Wins and Woes: Being part of a plant community, whether local or online, is like finding your tribe. You're no longer alone in obsessing over why snake plant doesn't grow or in celebrating the arrival of a new leaf on your Snake Plant. These spaces offer support, advice, and a sense of belonging.

Joining a plant community can vastly expand your plant knowledge. You'll learn new tips, discover rare plant species, and find solutions to problems you didn't even know existed. More importantly, you'll be surrounded by people who understand your excitement when that stubborn plant finally blooms.

Seek out local plant clubs, gardening workshops, or meetups. You can exchange plants, attend workshops, or simply connect with like-minded people over your shared love for all things green.

Many plant lovers find joy in giving back to their community through gardening. You might volunteer at a community garden, help with planting trees in your neighborhood, or even start a small plant library where people can take or leave plants. These actions not only beautify your surroundings but also help foster a greener, more connected community.

Plant Sharing as a Way of Life

A Greener, More Connected World:

Building a Legacy of Green: Sharing plants can become a way of life. Every plant you give away, every cutting you trade, contributes to a larger, greener network of people who care about the earth. This ripple effect means that with each act of sharing, you're helping to create a more sustainable, nature-focused community.

Spreading Positivity: There's something truly uplifting about knowing that the little plant you gave away is now thriving in someone else's home. You've not only shared a piece of greenery but also a bit of happiness and positivity that will continue to grow with time.

Making the World a Little Greener, Together

From Your Home to the World: Your journey as a plant lover is not just about nurturing plants but also about nurturing relationships—whether it's through gifting, swapping, or joining a community. As you share your passion, you'll realize that plants are more than just decorative items; they're bridges that connect us to each other and to the natural world.

With this chapter, you now understand that sharing plants isn't just about growing a collection—it's about spreading joy, building relationships, and contributing to a greener world. Each plant you share carries with it the potential to grow something much larger than itself. So go ahead, share the joy of plants, and watch how your small green acts make the world a little brighter.

Section 3: Mastering the Art of Gardening (Expert Gardeners)

Chapter 10
Advanced Plant Care Techniques

You've come a long way from your first plant, and by now, you've probably encountered every obstacle from drooping leaves to stubborn pests. But you've also experienced the incredible rewards of your plant journey—the thrill of new growth, the pride of nurturing a healthy plant, and maybe even a home bursting with greenery. Now, it's time to take your skills to the next level. In this section, we'll explore the art and science of advanced plant care. We're talking about growing rare plants, trying out innovative techniques, and even designing your dream garden, indoors or out.

If you're ready to level up your plant game, you're in the right place. This chapter is all about diving deeper into the methods that allow you to not just care for plants but master them.

Embracing Hydroponics: The Future of Plant Care

What is Hydroponics? Imagine growing your plants without soil. That's Hydroponics in a nutshell—using water, nutrients, and a growing medium like pebbles or coconut coir to support the plants. It's not just for science labs or futuristic greenhouses; it's a technique you can easily bring into your home.

Why try Hydroponics? The answer is simple. It's space-saving, efficient, and perfect for clean, modern indoor gardening. You'll also have more control over the nutrients your plants receive, leading to faster growth and healthier plants.

Getting Started: Setting up a hydroponic system might sound intimidating, but it's simpler than you think. Start small, with easy plants like herbs, and gradually expand your system as you get comfortable. Before long, you'll be growing lush basil, crisp lettuce, or even strawberries right on your kitchen counter!

Method 1: Wick System Hydroponics

This is one of the simplest forms of hydroponics, perfect for beginners. It involves placing a plant in a container with a wick that draws nutrient-rich water up from a reservoir to feed the plant.

Example Plants: Lettuce, herbs like basil, and houseplants such as Spider plants adapt well to wick systems.

Care: Ensure that the wick remains moist at all times and monitor the nutrient levels in the water.

Method 2: Deep Water Culture (DWC)

In this system, plant roots are suspended in a solution of water and nutrients, with an air pump supplying oxygen. This method allows for rapid growth.

Example Plants: Leafy greens like spinach, and houseplants like bamboo and money plants .

Care: Regularly change the water every 2-3 weeks and monitor pH levels to keep the solution balanced.

Building Your Own Terrarium: A Miniature World

What's a Terrarium? Think of a terrarium as a tiny ecosystem in a glass jar. These miniature gardens are not only beautiful but also a great way to showcase your creativity. They're perfect for small spaces and require little maintenance, making them an excellent project for plant lovers of all levels.

Creating Your Terrarium: Start by choosing a glass container—anything from a simple jar to a custom-made glass dome. Add layers of soil, charcoal, and pebbles, then select small plants from succulents family. The key to a successful terrarium is choosing plants that thrive in the same environment, so that they co-exist happily.

Caring for Your Little World: Terrariums are fairly self-sustaining but do require occasional attention. You'll need to monitor moisture levels, prune plants that grow too large, and ensure that your little ecosystem doesn't get too crowded.

Method 1: Open Terrarium

Best for plants that prefer dry conditions, such as succulents and cacti. Open terrariums allow for air circulation.

Example Plants: Aloe vera, snake plant and money plant.

Care: Place the terrarium in bright, indirect light and water sparingly.

Chapter 11

Cultivating Rare and Exotic Plants

Caring for rare and exotic plants is an adventure for those who want to expand their plant collection with species that are not commonly found. Although these plants often require unique conditions, they offer extraordinary rewards.

1. Carnivorous Plants

These fascinating plants thrive in nutrient-poor soils and have evolved to capture and digest insects to supplement their diets.

Example 1: Venus Flytrap

Native to subtropical wetlands, this plant catches insects with its jaw-like leaves.

Care: Requires bright, direct sunlight and filtered water. Never feed it anything other than insects.

Example 2: Pitcher Plant

With its tall, tube-like leaves filled with digestive enzymes, this plant captures insects by luring them in with sweet nectar.

Care: Prefers bright, indirect light and high humidity. Water with distilled water and keep in a moist environment.

2. Epiphytic Plants

Epiphytes are plants that grow on other plants rather than in soil. They absorb moisture and nutrients through their leaves from the air and rain.

Example 1: Staghorn Fern

This plant is often mounted on wooden boards or hung in baskets, resembling stag antlers.

Care: Needs indirect light and frequent misting. Soak the root ball in water weekly.

Example 2: Tillandsia (Air Plants)

These are some of the easiest epiphytes to care for, often used in creative displays without soil.

Care: Mist regularly and soak in water every 1-2 weeks. Ensure good air circulation.

3. Orchids

Growing orchids at home might sound a bit fancy, but trust me, it's easier than you think! These elegant beauties just need a few basics to thrive indoors.

First, lighting is key. Orchids love bright, indirect sunlight. Place them near a window that gets good light but not too much direct sun, or they'll get scorched. If the leaves start looking yellow, it's their way of saying, "Too much sun!"

When it comes to watering, less is more. Overwatering is a big no-no for orchids. A good rule of thumb is to water once a week, letting the roots dry out in between. Orchids are tropical, so they enjoy a humid environment. If your home is a bit dry, try misting them occasionally or placing the pot on a tray with pebbles and water to increase humidity.

As for potting, orchids need a well-draining mix like bark, coconut shells or sphagnum moss, not regular potting soil. This keeps their roots healthy and prevents rot. And don't forget to fertilize! A little vermicompost every couple of weeks during their growing season (just after monsoons) will help them bloom beautifully.

With a little care and attention, your orchids will reward you with stunning blooms that can last for months. It's like having a living piece of art in your home!

Chapter 12

Giving Back to Nature

Sustainability is a vital part of gardening. As expert gardeners, we can make choices that not only benefit our plants but also contribute to environmental conservation.

Composting at Home

Composting is one of the easiest ways to reduce waste and create nutrient-rich soil for your garden.

Method 1: Traditional Composting

Use kitchen scraps like vegetable peels, coffee grounds, and eggshells, combined with yard waste to create rich compost over time.

Care: Turn your compost pile regularly and ensure a balance of green and brown materials for decomposition.

Method 2: Vermicomposting

This method involves using worms to break down organic matter into compost. Worm bins are compact and can be kept indoors.

Care: Keep the bin moist and feed the worms regularly. Harvest the compost when it becomes rich and dark.

CREATING WILDLIFE HABITATS

Gardening can support local wildlife by providing food, shelter, and nesting materials.

Example 1: Pollinator Gardens

Plant flowers like lavender, mustard attract bees, butterflies, and other pollinators.

Care: Avoid pesticides, and plant native species to support local ecosystems.

Example 2: Bird-Friendly Gardens

Provide food sources like berries, seeds, and nectar-producing plants to attract birds.

Care: Install bird baths and nesting boxes to support bird populations year-round.

Chapter 13

Unusual Plant Care Hacks and Experiments

Are you ready to unlock the more curious side of plant care? In this chapter, we'll explore some quirky but effective plant care hacks and experiments that may surprise you! We'll dive into household items that work wonders, creative indoor hydroponic systems, fun plant communication experiments, and even techniques for keeping your plants clean and healthy with leaf cleaning and showering. Let's explore the unconventional side of plant love!

USING HOUSEHOLD ITEMS FOR PLANT CARE

You'd be amazed at how many things lying around your kitchen can be put to good use in your plant care routine. Some of these might sound strange, but they're backed by gardeners around the world!

Banana Peels: Nature's Fertilizer

Banana peels are rich in potassium, which helps your plants develop strong roots and resist disease. Chop them up and bury them in the soil, or steep them in water for a few days to create "banana tea" for your plants. Use this banana water once every few weeks to nourish your plants. It's especially helpful for flowering plants that need a little extra boost to produce blooms.

Onion Peels: A Nutrient Powerhouse

Don't throw away your onion peels! They're loaded with calcium, magnesium, potassium, and iron. Boil the peels in water, let the mixture cool, and use this nutrient-rich water to feed your plants. Onion peel water is particularly effective for boosting the health of leafy greens and promoting root growth. Use this water during your regular watering routine, about once every two weeks.

Rice and Lentil Wash Water: A Gentle Tonic

The water you use to rinse rice or lentils is full of starch and proteins, which helps plants absorb nutrients more efficiently. It's like giving them a gentle tonic. Next time you rinse rice or lentils, save that water and use it to water your plants. This hack is particularly beneficial for houseplants and potted herbs. It's mild enough to be used weekly, giving your plants a steady supply of nutrients.

Vegetable Peels: Compost in the Making

Instead of tossing vegetable peels like potato skins, carrot tops, or cucumber peels, compost them! If you're not ready to set up a full composting system, you can just put them in a water pot and pour this water onto all the plants after a couple of hours. You'll notice your plants will look happier and fuller with time.

Used Tea Leaves: A Balanced Booster

After enjoying your tea, save those used leaves—they're packed with nitrogen and can help improve soil structure. You can sprinkle the used tea leaves directly on the soil or mix them in. This is especially beneficial for acid-loving plants like ferns, roses, and hydrangeas. Just remember to avoid using tea that has been sweetened or flavored, as those additives can harm your plants.

Used squeezed lemon

A thumb rule to remember would be to know that all flowering or colored foliage plants need acidic soil to bloom. While all non-flowering plants do not need acidic soil.

So, after you squeeze out the lemon juice, just put the squeezed lemon in a mug of water for 12-24 hours. Next day just dilute it in 1:20 ratio and give your flowering plants a tonic to bloom.

Buttermilk: A Microbial Treat for Plants

Buttermilk may seem like an unusual plant food, but it can provide essential microorganisms that help break down organic matter in the soil, making nutrients more accessible to plants. Dilute buttermilk in water (one part buttermilk to ten parts water) and use this solution to water your plants every few weeks. Buttermilk is particularly beneficial for boosting the health of flowering plants and keeping the soil rich and fertile.

These kitchen hacks not only reduce waste but also give your plants a steady supply of natural nutrients, ensuring they thrive without the need for synthetic fertilizers. Whether you're brewing a nutrient-packed tea with onion peels or giving your plants a gentle tonic with rice water, these methods are simple yet effective ways to keep your plants happy and healthy.

The Power of Companion Planting Indoors

Companion planting isn't just for outdoor gardens. Some plants make great buddies indoors too, helping each other thrive. Let's pair a few for the perfect indoor synergy:

Example 1: Aloe Vera and Money Plant Lavender

Aloe Vera is known for its healing properties, while Money Plant for its grace t. Placing them together creates a magic duo that promotes both relaxation and health in your home. Aloe's water-retaining properties complement lavender's need for slightly drier conditions.

Example 2: Snake Plants and Orchids

These two plants love humidity, making them perfect companions in a bathroom or a humid room. The Snake plant helps absorb harmful chemical compounds from the air, benefiting the more delicate orchid, which needs just the right level of clean air and humidity to thrive.

Example 3: Spider Plants and Peace Lilies

These two air-purifying powerhouses do well together, improving the air quality in your home while adding lush greenery. Spider plants love indirect light, while Peace Lilies prefer shade, making them perfect partners in spaces with variable lighting.

Plant Leaves Cleaning and Showering

Just like us, plants need a little cleaning to stay healthy and look their best. Dust and grime can block sunlight and inhibit growth, so it's important to keep those leaves clean.

Wiping Down Leaves

For plants with larger leaves, a gentle wipe-down can make all the difference. Use a soft cloth dampened with water or a mixture of water and a few drops of coconut oil. If your foliage is dirty -

use mild soap with water to wipe at first followed by wiping again with a cloth dampened in clean water and coconut oil. Gently wipe the leaves from top to bottom, making sure to remove dust and any buildup. You can feel your leaves and the entire plant smiling back at you.

Showering Your Plants

Smaller plants or those with many leaves, like ferns and spider plants, love a good shower. Place them in your bathtub or sink and gently rinse them with lukewarm water. This not only cleans the leaves but also helps keep pests at bay. Just be careful not to drench plants that don't like too much water—make sure they're in well-draining pots!

There you have it—some unusual but exciting plant care hacks and experiments that can add a new layer of fun and curiosity to your plant care routine. Whether you're soaking banana peels, setting up a hydroponic system in your kitchen, or chatting with your plants, remember that taking care of plants is all about creativity, exploration, and most importantly, enjoying the process.

Your green journey is far from over—there's always something new to discover! Keep experimenting and watch as your love for plants continues to grow.

Chapter 14

The Art of Plant Communication

As an expert gardener, you understand that plants are living beings that communicate their needs through subtle signs. This chapter explores the art of plant communication, helping you deepen your connection with your plants and respond to their needs more intuitively.

Reading Plant Signals

Plants communicate through their appearance, growth patterns, and even their scent. Learning to read these signals can help you address issues before they become serious problems.

Leaf Color and Texture: Changes in leaf color or texture often indicate a problem. Yellowing leaves may signal overwatering or nutrient deficiency, while crispy, brown edges can indicate underwatering or low humidity.

Growth Patterns: Slow or leggy growth can be a sign that your plant isn't getting enough light. Conversely, rapid, soft growth might indicate too much nitrogen or insufficient light.

Scent: Some plants release scents as a response to stress or as a way to attract pollinators. A change in scent can be an early warning sign of pests or disease.

Responding to Plant Needs

Once you've identified what your plant is communicating, it's important to respond appropriately. Here's how to address common issues:

Adjusting Light: If your plant is showing signs of light stress, adjust its location or provide supplemental lighting. For plants that need more light, consider using grow lights to mimic natural sunlight.

Modifying Watering Practices: Pay attention to the soil's moisture level and adjust your watering schedule accordingly. If your plant is overwatered, allow the soil to dry out completely before watering again. If underwatered, increase the frequency or amount of water.

Nutrient Management: If your plant is showing signs of nutrient deficiency, such as pale leaves or stunted growth, consider fertilizing with a vermicompost. Be careful not to over-fertilize, as this can cause more harm than good.

Building a Deep Connection: Beyond the practical aspects of plant care, developing a deeper connection with your plants can enhance your gardening experience and overall well-being.

Mindful Gardening: Practice mindfulness while caring for your plants. Take time to observe their growth, appreciate their beauty, and connect with the natural world. This can reduce stress and increase your sense of fulfillment.

Rituals and Routines: Establishing rituals or routines in your plant care can strengthen your bond with your plants. Whether it's a morning walk through your garden or a weekly watering routine, these rituals create a sense of harmony and rhythm.

Chapter 15

A Lifelong Love for Plants

Congratulations! You've reached the final chapter of the first part of your plant adventure. Whether you've just discovered the joy of nurturing your first snake plant or are already experimenting with advanced care techniques, this chapter will help you reflect on what you've learned and inspire you to keep growing.

Reflecting on Your Journey

As you've navigated through Section 1, you've developed your green thumb by choosing your first plants and learning the basics of care. From understanding how water, light, and soil work together to creating a cozy green space, you've built a solid foundation. Remember, each plant you've cared for has been a small victory and a step towards becoming a more confident gardener.

Section 2 expanded your knowledge and confidence, introducing you to a variety of plants and how to handle common challenges. You've learned how to tackle pests, diseases, and how to repot and propagate. You've also discovered how to design beautiful plant displays and share your passion with others. Your growing collection of plants is a testament to your dedication and enthusiasm.

In Section 3, you took your skills to the next level by mastering advanced techniques and exploring the art of designing both indoor and outdoor gardens. Whether you were experimenting with hydroponics or cultivating rare and exotic plants, you've embraced new challenges and learned innovative ways to enhance your green spaces. Your journey has equipped you with the knowledge and creativity to turn any space into a thriving garden.

Looking Forward: Your Next Green Adventure

As you move forward, remember that gardening is a continuous journey of learning and discovery. Every plant has its own story, and each new addition to your collection brings new opportunities for growth. Here are a few ways to keep your green adventure going:

- **Experiment and Explore:** Don't be afraid to try new techniques or plant varieties. Whether it's starting a new hydroponic system or experimenting with companion planting, every experiment adds to your gardening expertise.
- **Connect with Fellow Gardeners:** Join plant communities, both online and offline. Sharing experiences, advice, and plant swaps can provide new perspectives and inspiration. Engaging with others who share your passion can be both motivating and rewarding.
- **Continue Learning:** There's always more to discover in the world of gardening. Read books, attend workshops, or follow gardening blogs to keep expanding your knowledge. Each new piece of information can help you become a better gardener.
- **Reflect and Adapt:** Regularly assess your gardening practices and reflect on what's working and what could be improved. Adapting your methods based on your

experiences will help you create a more flourishing and harmonious green space.

A Lifelong Love for Plants

Gardening is more than just a hobby; it's a passion that grows with you. As you've learned from the basics of plant care to mastering advanced techniques, remember that there's always more to explore. Plants have a way of teaching us patience, creativity, and resilience. Each plant you care for and each new gardening challenge you tackle enriches your experience and deepens your connection to nature. Embrace the journey with curiosity and enthusiasm, knowing that the world of plants will continue to surprise and delight you.

To close, let's draw inspiration from seasoned plant lovers who have shared their wisdom and passion:

"The love of gardening is a seed once sown that never dies." — Gertrude Jekyll

"Plants give us oxygen for the lungs and for the soul." — Anonymous

"Gardening adds years to your life and life to your years." — Anonymous

These words remind us that gardening is a source of both physical and emotional nourishment. It's a journey filled with moments of joy, learning, and growth. As you continue to nurture your plants and garden, let these inspirations guide you and keep your passion alive.

Thank you for joining me on this green adventure. May your plants always thrive, and may your garden be a source of joy and inspiration for years to come.

Happy gardening!